MW00882164

# Dad and Me: Our Back and Forth Prompted Journal and Adventure Log Book

# Dad and Me: Our Back and Forth Prompted Journal and Adventure Log Book for kids

## With Interview Questions, Family Tree, Family History, and Adventures to Connect and Bond

Merri Bithiah Boyson

**Dad and Me: Our Back and Forth Prompted Journal**

Copyright ©2021 by Merri Boyson. All rights reserved. No part of this book may be reproduced in any form or by any electronic or mechanical means including information storage or retrieval systems without prior written permission of the copyright owner. Merri.Boyson@gmail.com. First Edition

# Table of Contents

Me and Dad................................................................7

About My Grandparents.........................................45

Adventures ...............................................................50

Take A Hike .............................................................51

Visit A Historical Site ............................................53

Go Bowling...............................................................55

Visit A Museum ......................................................57

Go Skating ...............................................................59

Go Fishing ...............................................................61

Go Camping ............................................................63

Movie Time .............................................................65

Go Stargazing .........................................................67

Visit A Veterans Museum ....................................69

Picnic Time .............................................................71

Have A Dance Party ..............................................73

# Table of Contents

Go Swimming ...................................................................75

Family Tree ....................................................................77

About My Great Grandparents .............................................78

Junior Ranger Badge ........................................................ 86

Go To A Play ..................................................................87

Treasure Hunt ................................................................89

Mini-Golf ......................................................................90

Visit A Zoo ....................................................................91

Plant A Garden ...............................................................93

Visit A Library ................................................................95

Build A Fort ...................................................................96

Review .........................................................................97

## My name is

_____

I am _____ years old

My birthday is _____

The date today is _____

7

Me

I live in this city: _____

I am in this grade: _____

My teacher is: _____

I go to school by: _____

# This is a picture of me.

9

Dad

# Dad, what is your full legal name?

_____

How old are you?_____

What is your birthday?_____

where were your born? _____

what hospital were your born in?

_____

What city, state, and country were you born in?

_____

What did your parent's call you?_____

Did your friends give you any nickname?_____

Have you changed your name since you were born?

_____

Dad

# This is a picture of Dad.

# These are my family members

Me

_____

_____

_____

_____

_____

_____

13

Me          # This is a picture of my family

# Who were the people in your family when you were my age?

_____     _____

_____     _____

_____     _____

_____     _____

_____     _____

_____     _____

Dad

what is your earliest memory? _____
_____

where did you grow up? _____

what was your home like? _____
_____
_____
_____
_____
_____

# Three things I like to do in school are

1. _____

2. _____

3. _____

Dad

# Name three things you liked in school.

1. _____

2. _____

3. _____

# SOME OF MY
# FAVORITE THINGS

**MY FAVORITE COLOR**_____

**MY FAVORITE FOOD**_____

**MY FAVORITE BOOK**_____

**MY FAVORITE SPORT/ACTIVITY** _____

**MY FAVORITE ANIMAL**_____

19

Dad

# SOME OF MY DAD'S FAVORITE THINGS

**FAVORITE COLOR** _____

**FAVORITE FOOD** _____

**FAVORITE BOOK** _____

**FAVORITE SPORT/ACTIVITY** _____

**FAVORITE ANIMAL** _____

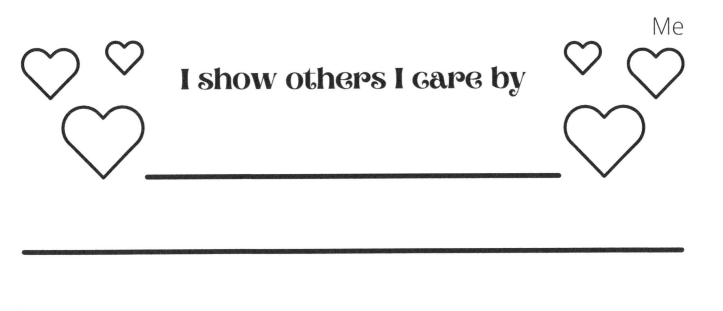

# I show others I care by

_____

_____

_____

Dad

# Dad, how do you show others you care?

_____

_____

_____

## Things I like about me

_____

_____

_____

Dad

SUPER

Dad, what do you like about you?

_____

_____

_____

# what was your favorite childhood memory?

_____

_____

_____

# what were your favorite toys? _____

_____

# what games did you like to play? _____

_____

# what sports did you play as a kid? _____

_____

Me

# My favorite things to do with you are

# My Favorite Memory With You

Me

# My favorite memory with you, Dad, is

_____

_____

_____

_____

_____

# Dad, what is your favorite memory of you and me?

_____

_____

_____

_____

_____

_____

# My favorite things we do as a family are

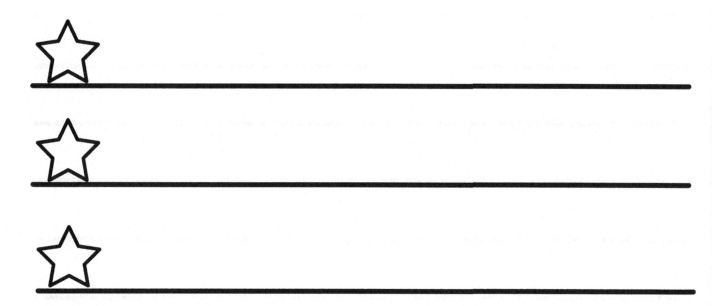

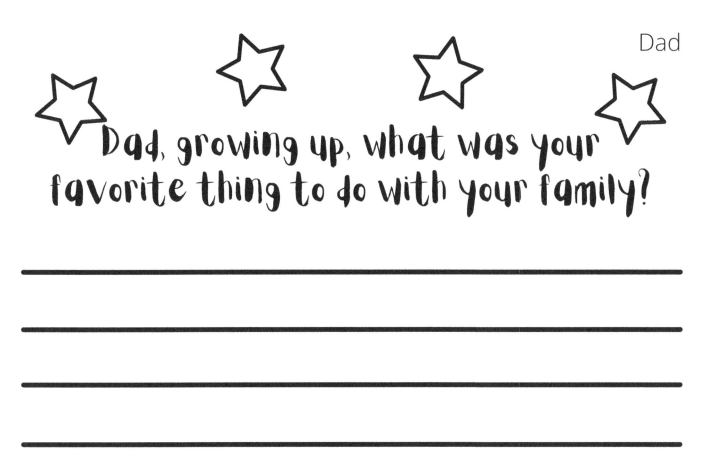

Dad, growing up, what was your favorite thing to do with your family?

_____

_____

_____

_____

# Some things I would like to do as a family are

_____

_____

_____

# Dad, what are some things you would like for us to do as a family?

_____

_____

_____

# My favorite season of the year is

## I like it because

_____

_____

# Dad, what is your favorite season of the year?

## what do you like about it?

_____

_____

Me

# My favorite holiday is

# I like it because

Dad
# what is your favorite holiday?

# what do you like about it?

# My favorite family traditions we do for holidays are

1 _____

2 _____

3 _____

Dad, when you were growing up, what were your favorite family traditions you did for the holidays?

1 _____

2 _____

3 _____

# My favorite place that I have been

## I liked it because

_____

_____

_____

_____

# what is your favorite place that you have been?

## what did you like about it?

Dad

# what were your favorite things there?

_____

_____

_____

_____

what is your father's full name?

_____

what is his birthday? _____

where was he born? _____

Do you know what hospital he was born in? _____

what is his nationality? _____

what did he do for work? _____

# what is your favorite memory with your dad?

---

---

# what was one of your favorite things to do with your dad?

---

---

# what is your mother's full name?

_____

what is her birthday? _____

where was she born? _____

Do you know what hospital she was
born in? _____

what is her nationality? _____

what did she do for work? _____

Dad

# what is your favorite memory with your mom?

_____

_____

# what was one of your favorite things to do with your mom?

_____

_____

# what was a typical day like in your house when you were a kid?

_____

_____

_____

_____

_____

_____

_____

_____

# Adventures

# Take a Hike

DATE _____   DISTANCE _____

Location/Park _____

Trail Name _____

Difficulty          easy   1   2   3   4   5   hard

The trail was paved/cleared/marked

Hiking partners _____

_____

# Hiking Notes

## WHAT DID I SEE ON THE TRAIL?

Dad
_____

_____

Me
_____

_____

# Visit a Historical Site

## PLACE: _____

### DATE: _____

## WHAT HAPPENED AT THIS PLACE?

Dad _____

_____

_____

# Art: Historical Site

# Go Bowling!

## Bowling Score Sheet

| NAME | 1 | 2 | 3 | 4 | 5 | 6 | 7 | 8 | 9 | 10 | TOTAL |
|------|---|---|---|---|---|---|---|---|---|----|-------|
| 01 | | | | | | | | | | | |
| 02 | | | | | | | | | | | |
| 03 | | | | | | | | | | | |
| 04 | | | | | | | | | | | |
| 05 | | | | | | | | | | | |
| 06 | | | | | | | | | | | |
| 07 | | | | | | | | | | | |

| 08 | | | | | | | | | | |
| 09 | | | | | | | | | | |
| 10 | | | | | | | | | | |
| 11 | | | | | | | | | | |
| 12 | | | | | | | | | | |
| 13 | | | | | | | | | | |
| 14 | | | | | | | | | | |
| 15 | | | | | | | | | | |
| 16 | | | | | | | | | | |

# VISIT A MUSEUM

**DATE**

**MUSEUM NAME**

**LOCATION**

# WHAT DID YOU LIKE?

Dad
_____

_____

_____

Me
_____

_____

_____

Date_____

# *Go*
# *Skating*

Me

# *Skating Art*

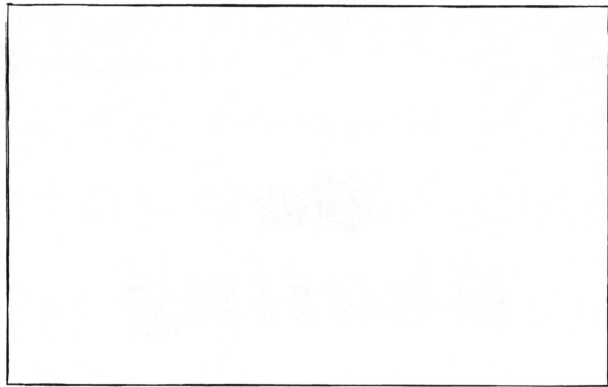

# *Go*
# *Fishing*
## FISHING *Log*

| DATE: | | START: | FINISH: |
|---|---|---|---|
| LOCATION: | | | |
| GPS: | | PARTNER: | |
| COMPANIONS: | | | |

## WEATHER & WATER

| AIR TEMP | WATER TEMP | WATER LEVEL | CLARITY | MOON |
|---|---|---|---|---|
| | | | | |

## CATCH LOG

| | SPECIES | W/L/G | KEPT | LURE | BAIL | METHOD |
|---|---|---|---|---|---|---|
| **Me** | | | | | | |
| | | | | | | |
| | | | | | | |
| | | | | | | |
| | | | | | | |
| **Dad** | | | | | | |
| | | | | | | |
| | | | | | | |
| | | | | | | |
| | | | | | | |

# CAMPING

## Go camping in your living room, backyard, or a camp site

Dad

Where did you camp? _____

What was the weather? _____

Date? _____

What did we do? _____

_____

Me

# What was your favorite part of camping?

# Make Your Favorite Snacks and Have a Movie Night

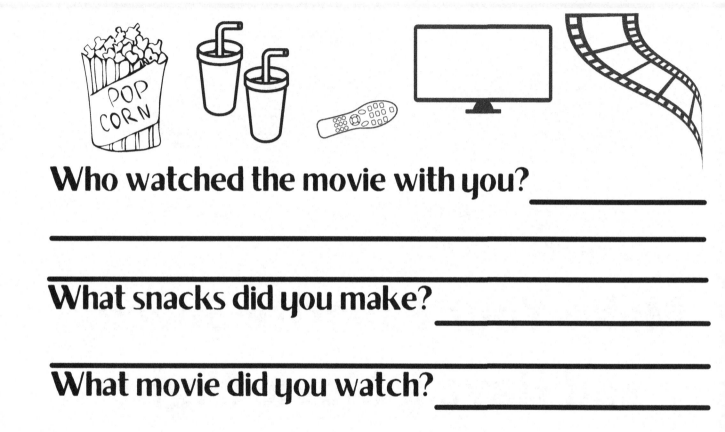

**Who watched the movie with you?** _____

_____

**What snacks did you make?** _____

**What movie did you watch?** _____

_____

# Go Stargazing

**Date** _____

### What are the names of the constellations you found?

_____  _____

_____  _____

_____  _____

# What constellations did you find?

## Draw the constellations you found?

Dad and me

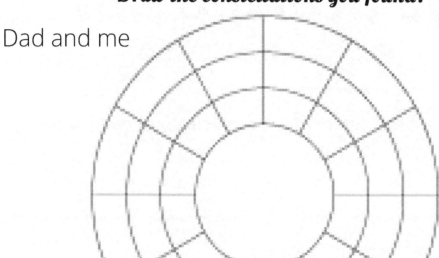

# VISIT A VETERANS MUSEUM

Dad

**WHAT DID YOU SEE?** _____

_____

_____

**WHAT DID YOU LEARN?** _____

_____

_____

Me

**WHAT DID YOU SEE?** _____

_____

_____

**WHAT DID YOU LEARN?** _____

_____

_____

_____

# Have a picnic at a park

Me

# Draw a picture of your picnic

# Have a Dance Party!

## FAVORITE SONGS PLAYED

Dad

Me

_____  _____

_____  _____

_____  _____

_____  _____

_____  _____

73

# SONGS PLAYED

Dad

Me

AT THE *pool*

# Go Swimming

Dad and me

# What was your favorite thing you did at the pool?

# Complete the Family Tree

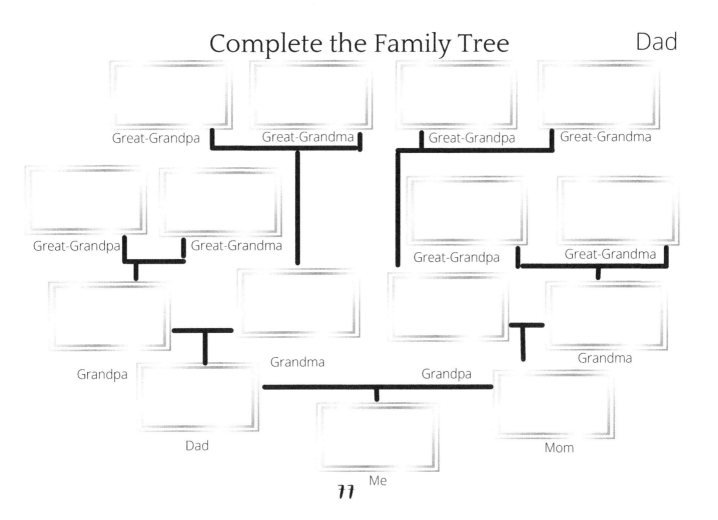

Great-Grandpa

Great-Grandma

Great-Grandpa

Great-Grandma

Great-Grandpa

Great-Grandma

Great-Grandpa

Great-Grandma

Grandpa

Grandma

Grandpa

Grandma

Dad

Mom

Me

77

Dad

Dad, what is your paternal grandfather's
full name? _____
What did you call him? _____
What is his birthday? _____
Where was he born? _____
Do you know what hospital he was
born in? _____

What is his nationality? _____
What did he do for work? _____

# what is your favorite memory with your grandfather?

_____

_____

# what was one of your favorite things to do with your grandfather?

_____

_____

_____

Dad

Dad, what is your paternal grandmother's full name? _____

what did you call her? _____

what is her birthday? _____

where was she born? _____

Do you know what hospital she was born in? _____

what is her nationality? _____

what did she do for work? _____

# what is your favorite memory with your grandmother?

_____

# what was one of your favorite things to do with your grandmother?

_____

_____

Dad, what is your maternal grandfather's full name? _____

What did you call him? _____

What is his birthday? _____

Where was he born? _____

Do you know what hospital he was born in? _____

What is his nationality? _____

What did he do for work? _____

# what is your favorite memory with your grandfather?

# what was one of your favorite things to do with your grandfather?

Dad, what is your maternal grandmother's full name? _____

What did you call her? _____

What is her birthday? _____

Where was she born? _____

Do you know what hospital she was born in? _____

What is her nationality? _____

What did she do for work? _____

# what is your favorite memory with your grandmother?

_____

_____

# what was one of your favorite things to do with your grandmother?

_____

_____

_____

# VISIT A NATIONAL PARK

Visit the National Park Service website at www.nps.gov to find national parks.
Or, complete a Junior Ranger Badge online at National Parks Service Junior Ranger Program. There are pages and pages of different badges that can be completed.

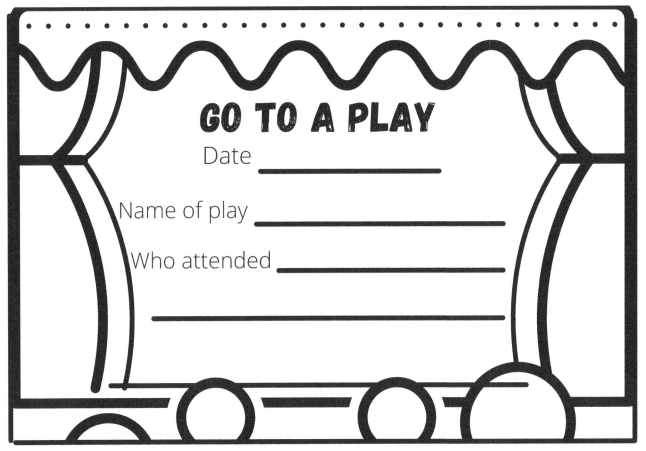

# GO TO A PLAY

Date _____

Name of play _____

Who attended _____

_____

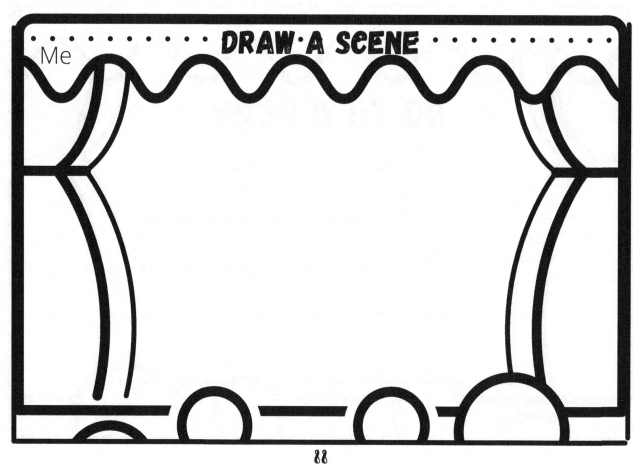

DRAW·A·SCENE

Me

# Explore an Attic, Basement, or Closet for Family Treasures

## What did you find?

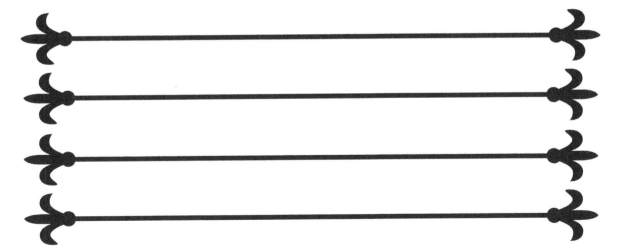

# Play Mini-Golf

Date _____

| Players | 1 | 2 | 3 | 4 | 5 | 6 | 7 | 8 | 9 | 10 | 11 | 12 | 13 | 14 | 15 | 16 | 17 | 18 | score |
|---------|---|---|---|---|---|---|---|---|---|----|----|----|----|----|----|----|----|----|-------|
|         |   |   |   |   |   |   |   |   |   |    |    |    |    |    |    |    |    |    |       |
|         |   |   |   |   |   |   |   |   |   |    |    |    |    |    |    |    |    |    |       |
|         |   |   |   |   |   |   |   |   |   |    |    |    |    |    |    |    |    |    |       |
|         |   |   |   |   |   |   |   |   |   |    |    |    |    |    |    |    |    |    |       |
|         |   |   |   |   |   |   |   |   |   |    |    |    |    |    |    |    |    |    |       |
|         |   |   |   |   |   |   |   |   |   |    |    |    |    |    |    |    |    |    |       |

91

# What's your favorite animal?

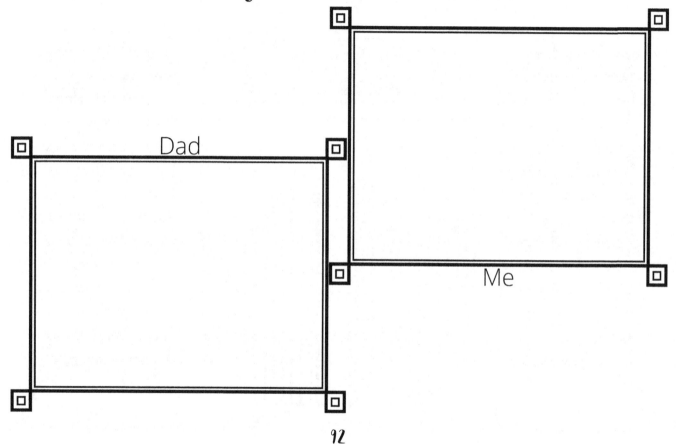

Dad

Me

# Plant a Garden

Dad and me

## Layout your garden

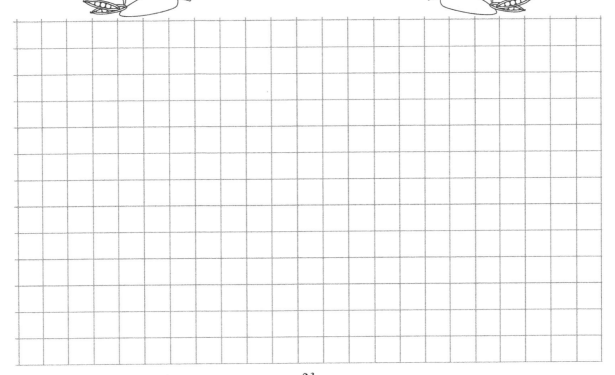

Dad and me

# Garden Journal

Plant

| | Today's Date | Planting Depth | Spacing | Thin to | Days to Harvest | Harvest Dates | How did the plants do: Notes |
|---|---|---|---|---|---|---|---|
| | | | | | | | |
| | | | | | | | |
| | | | | | | | |
| | | | | | | | |
| | | | | | | | |
| | | | | | | | |

# VISIT A LIBRARY
## MAKE A READING LIST

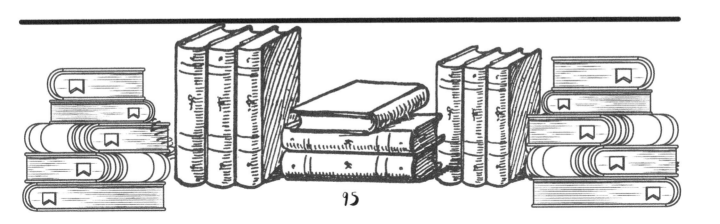

Dad and me

# Build a Fort and Watch a Movie or Read a Book

Date _____

What did you watch or read? _____

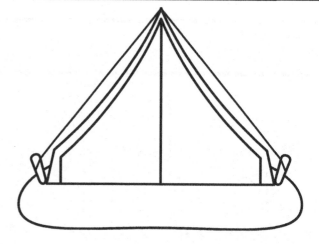

Looking back, what are your favorite activities you've done together?

## About the Author

Merri Boyson is the mother of three grown children and the grandmother to three great kids. A native of Ohio, she grew up in Texas, and now lives in West Virginia. She works as an Advocate and spends her spare time finding adventures of her own.

Look for new books from Merri Boyson, including Dad and Me: Our Back and Forth Prompted Journal and Adventure Log Book for Teens with more family history, planning for the future you want, and career exploration, and more adventures to connect and bond.

Made in the USA
Monee, IL
14 June 2021

71237008R00057